# THE
# AWAKENING
# OF
# FRIENDSHIP

A Spiritual Journey Embracing Our Family of Friends
with Healing Affirmations

# THE AWAKENING
# OF FRIENDSHIP

Carol Olivia Adams

While all of the stories in this book are true, the names and personal characteristics of the individuals involved have been changed in order to protect the privacy and deep respect of the client. Any resulting resemblance to another person, living or dead, is entirely coincidental and totally unintentional.

Copyright © 2015 Carol Olivia Adams

Library of Congress control no. 2015917696

CreateSpace Independent Publishing Platform
North Charleston, SC

ISBN: 13: 978-1516950447
ISBN: 10: 1516950445

TO

THE LOVING PLAN OF THE

CREATOR.

I HONOR YOUR WISDOM.

# Contents

## Song for The Awakening of Friendship

Song of friendship is gracious
Sings inside and sings out
And below and up high

The same air that lifts the eagle's wing
Is the breeze that lights the dove
Is the wind that flies the song
With the Creator up above

And down below our feet
The same air moves within the ground
Where water, rock, and roots run deep
The air circles the song around

The heart that sings has heard the song
Shhh—listen to the air
The song of friendship is gracious
Is singing everywhere

**Carol Olivia Adams**

# Acknowledgements

I am most appreciative of the talented, patient, and insightful editor, Mark Russell Reed.

I want to acknowledge writers Anthony Shields and Juliana Adams, both spontaneous writers.

I treasure the love, intellect, and loyalty of my brother, my friend Dr. George Gabriel Adams.

I am forever grateful for the angelic love, kindness, and nurturing of my friend Joan Marie Bacon.

I embrace the friendship of Brittany Bacon, wise, and supportive.

I hold dear to my heart the consistent friendship of Dr. Anna Bettios, Paul Arida and Amelia and Stan.

And Stan Hillhouse, photographer and friend for consistently reminding me of the value of the book and how it helps to serve mankind.

I respect the alternative healers and medical professionals who guided my spirit, all for the advancement of my calling.

There are so many more friendships, beginning with the compassion of Rudy and Martha Gonzales, Steve Cocoras, Karen, Nadine, Lora, Andrew, supportive and caring Rich Z. and Pam Tournier who have embraced me over the years. I want to thank each of you and many more loving friends who have touched my heart and shed light into my soul. I will never forget any one of you.

My heart will always honor the signs of the Creator, who continuously guides me along my road trip of life. I acknowledge our spiritual friendship.

# INTRODUCTION

In the earlier years of my life, I used to envision a field of flowers dancing to the rhythm of the wind with the blazing sun comforting each petal as it opened up to the world. Each flower would become my friend and each petal hugged me with love in its heart. Each friendship became a loving source of the light, the radiance, and the powerful voice of the Creator.

Many years ago, I was born just like you, a creation nurtured from the Infinite Source who had silently given me the opportunity to blossom to my fullest potential within the road trip of life. The soul knew that I wished to endure, honor my freedom, and attain wisdom. My cry to the universe proclaimed the celebration to life. Life is a school of lessons and I was determined to graduate with honors. My psyche chose this spiritual contract and I was willing to learn through all of the events, good and ugly. The soul was also aware that this divine miracle was a manifestation emanating from the love of the Infinite, reflecting a spiritual partnership written in stone.

I began my journey. My parents passed on when I was at a young age. The difficulties of these events punctured my fragile heart, creating much confusion about the purpose of my existence. My spirit became lifeless and my soul became fragmented, like the growing lack of harmony in the divine universe.

A couple of family members tried to extend themselves during these delicate and precious times but the glass still needed to be filled. I then realized the importance of the human connection, the spiritual nutrition that would nurture the body, mind, and spirit.

My own journey became very apparent to me. Reality knocked at the door like a loud bellow. I was forced to engage with a world which had supplied me with feelings of isolation and despair. Nevertheless, I desired to survive triumphantly and this enlightenment propelled my spirit to soar. I became grounded to the total presence of life without any thread of illusion. I became courageous in my plight, my heart's desire, and my mission to serve people. Spirituality became the priority of my journey, an inner faith with the Divine trusting the steps that were given to me, positive and negative. I was alone and lonely, and this awareness stirred within me a strong creative spirit, the perseverance of my beliefs, and the respect of my full identity. I AM CAROL OLIVIA ADAMS.

I am sure that some of you have experienced rough situations in the passages of your lives. You may have turned to blood ties only to receive limited loving response, action, or compassion. You then delved into your needs, enlightening you to a newer perspective of a family. This manifested a new formula for a family, of loving human beings who would extend their human hearts without hesitation. As you had endured these traumatic occurrences, I also hoped to embrace loving human beings, nurturers who would also enhance my calling and spiritual growth.

This self-realization of a family also inspired me to become the human being that the Creator had orchestrated for me. I wanted to blossom like the bouquet of pink roses: vibrant, gentle, and strong.

It did not matter to me the nature of the nurturer, family member or not. This wisdom paved the road for a new family of friends, blood relatives or not, who would nurture the blossoming of my soul with grace, kindness, compassion, and the essence of love. This new awareness became very precious and sacred to me, reflecting the infinite source of love, the Creator.

I had learned through all of these intense experiences that the word love was only one word and nothing more than that. I needed to feel the honesty of the person's voice within my heart and in my gut.

Just as I had cried at birth for the celebration of my soul to the universe, I also cried joyfully for the human experience of friendship. Maybe these heartbreaking incidents agitated my psyche to deeply meditate on the meaning and the need for a family of friends or human beings that would mirror the principles of humanity as well as crystallize my soul. Maybe you the reader have related to this insight through the many passages of your journey.

During the following years, I was again challenged to evaluate the deeper meaning of friendship. I had a professional intuitive practice and spoke to hundreds and hundreds of clients. I became very aware of the importance of my patient ear, sincerity, and kindness during the process of healing and the connection to their human spirit. I intuitively listened to many stories of clients such as a client's becoming fearful of eviction from their property because of rent-control issues, bisexuals who became confused with their real sexuality, evaluating the proper milligram for the dosage of a vitamin, intuitively delving into the purchase of a specific type of orgonite, feeling the presence of a spirit, deciphering whether or not a relative poisoned their mother, guiding a client with their business pursuits, determining whether or not someone would be financially and morally worthwhile for a financial advisor, romance stories, and many more.

It became apparent to me that my clients needed an understanding human being to talk to without any ounce of intimidation. They needed a person they could proudly call their friend.

I intuitively felt deep in my heart that some clients had never exposed their stories to anyone but me. They had placed their trust in me, revealing the deep-rooted feelings and thoughts that were hidden in their soul over many, many years. I believe that the more we submerge any uncomfortable experience, the more we hide our truths. We subconsciously become fearful and insecure without knowing why we are so reluctant to go forward with the course of our journey. We become the snapping turtle and cautiously hide in our shell. This protective action diminishes the vitality of our spirit.

Over the years, I shed light to my clients with the human principles of patience, compassion, and the presence of listening, some of the human principles or awakenings of friendship that I mention in this book.

I became a trustworthy friend, a voice at the end of the phone who was always there for them, while listening and speaking to each client from the depth of my human heart. I nurtured each individual just as a flower needs the natural elements of water, the sacred land, and the warmth of the sun to grow to its fullest potential.

The interesting scenario is that we had never seen each other. The phone sessions were heart to heart. Friendships became genuine.

The more a client opened up to me, the more they embraced their courage and inner security, two more human principles or awakenings for the blossoming of friendship. The sessions became healing for both of us.

I will give you a few examples of how a caring friend heals the wounded soul.

Children in school who are from disadvantaged backgrounds need a comfort zone. A kind-hearted teacher can produce a gentle, non-intimidating environment which can increase the willingness to learn as well as stirring the flow of the child's creativity. The child intuits that the teacher is their friend, which is so meaningful for the advancement of their learning. Friendships are very important to children. I also believe that adversaries can propel a child or adult to try harder, especially when they know they have a caring human being by their side.

Another illustration is the setting of the patient and physician. I believe that the spirit, the vitality, the passion of the patient is so important and magical for the healing process. Many physicians are great doctors but are not good healers.

A compassionate doctor can nurture the patient with a positive attitude about their specific healing. Compassion is a spiritual medication. It is beautiful when a patient feels the human connection, because the more genuine or human the doctor is with the patient, the more they will open up to the health practitioner with all of their concerns. It will blossom into a working healing friendship.

During the years of my profession, I would receive many thank-you cards from my clients expressing their appreciation of our friendship. I have saved many cards in many shoe boxes.

I learned from them, as they learned from me, the human experience of friendship.

My clients are human beings, just like you, who simply need a caring friend to deeply express their baffling confusion, secret fears, and wishes to.

We all have something that is boiling in our system which we do not consciously understand. Maybe that child in the classroom just needed a direction in their lives, a hope or belief from a kind friend, a teacher.

A good friend can anoint the soul with the spiritual gifts of humanity. It is my sincere hope that the clients I served will always sing their own song, joyfully dance to the music of life, and walk with dignity in their hearts. I cherish our friendships.

Later on in my journey, I was challenged with an extremely difficult health issue. This trauma propelled me to reassess my friendships, discovering their authenticity, consistency of spiritual support, and capacity to embrace the golden thread of compassion.

The more my friends extended themselves to me physically, emotionally, and spiritually, the more they unknowingly connected to the depth of their heart and to the love of the Creator. It was their calling as well as mine to give love and to receive love to the best capacity, without any hesitation.

They were beckoned to become angels, to magically assist me in my healing process whether they knew it or not.

Friendships elevated my spirit during these rough times by embracing the awakening of patience, allowing me to heal on my own accord, and respecting my own unique timing, like the plant that grows in its own special way with temperance as its master tool. Patient friends became healers respecting the laws of nature and the laws of life.

My healing became spiritually dependent on the wisdom of patience as well as faith, another human principle or awakening in friendship. Faith was my spiritual tool. It ignited my spirit. Faith is a silent powerful voice. Loving friends who have faith in us respect exactly who we are and trust our foremost decisions without bearing judgment or criticism.

The more I saw the more I knew. The nine awakenings in this book suggest a calling for every human being to look into themselves and the human principles of friendship and to capture our light within, our golden thread of humanity.

Let me take you on a spiritual journey with *The Awakening of Friendship*.

— Carol Olivia Adams

## THE FIRST AWAKENING

## WISDOM OF PATIENCE

*With time and patience
the mulberry leaf becomes
a silk gown.*

— Chinese proverb

*Have patience. All things change
in due time. Wishing cannot bring
autumn glow nor cause winter to cease.*

— Cherokee

Patience is kind and sincere. It honors every moment and is as gentle as the warm summer breeze. Patience respects the steps of the divine process and allows each moment to unfold to the highest order that was intended by the Creator. It does not become impatient with the timing of the changes of the seasons or the opening of a blossoming flower. We cannot push the stages of Mother Nature nor can we change the developmental steps of friendship. People bound in friendship have their own expressions of transforming the friendship in the exact way that was orchestrated by the Creator.

Patience maintains an aura of peacefulness despite a windy storm. It is persistent and usually has a foreseen purpose. Patience recognizes that life is constant change and will always throw us the unexpected when we least expect it. Nature will transform just as different friends will enter into the different chapters of their lives.

The evolution of a meaningful friendship may not always be foreseen, just as the initial brushstroke of an artist will never reveal its fullest composition.

Georgia O'Keefe once illustrated…

> Nobody sees a flower — really — it is so
> small — we haven't time — and to see

takes time, like to have a friend takes
time …

The god-like colors of a flower are unsurpassed by
any artist's palette and the rest of its creation will
always be a mystery to mankind. We are not the
Master of this divine image, nor the conductor of its
spiritual order. The opening of the first petal beholds
its own process of timing within the cosmic mind
which is infinite.

Thomas Edison…

I never failed once. It just happened to
be a 2000-step process.

The gentle persistence of patience in friendship does
not waiver and our friend learns to trust and honor
our staying power. This experience encourages our
dear friend to open up their hearts and we wisely
listen to their intimate story.

This creates a deeper bonding and understanding.
We learn to accept our friend as a human being with
strengths and weaknesses and we formulate no
judgment. A patient friend enhances our healing and
he or she becomes our spiritual physician.

Albert Einstein reflected…

It's not that I am smart, it's just that I
stay with the problem longer.

## The Servicemen's Story

Patience was very important to some of my clients
who served in the military and it became the key
factor for their survival. The wisdom of patience was
their key tactic for victory. Sometimes, they would
rather wait it out than forge ahead. They learned more
of the enemy's strategy by remaining still.

These life challenges created an intimacy and
understanding between the men in combat. A family
of friends was created with the intention of protecting
each other from the enemy, no matter what the
circumstances or consequences.

They listened to each other's history with
compassion and insight and without discrimination.
They connected on a real human level with respect,
loyalty, and cooperation.

## Reflection:

Patience can be a key tactic for survival as well as
for gaining insight into the exact steps that are
given to us. Some of us like to rush while others
like to stop and smell the petals of the flower.
These servicemen needed the wisdom of patience

4

to survive, to be still and outsmart the enemy. True intimacy was created with the time to bond and to deeply understand their comrade. The heart of patience respects the other without discrimination. It allows the petals of the flower to open with its own accord.

These men learned to appreciate each other while creating their own family of friends. This also enhanced more harmony within themselves. This also allowed for better physical strategies allowing the enemy to advance while they remained still.

Patience is a virtue.

Leo Tolstoy once wrote…

The two most powerful warriors are patience and time.

## Pam's Story

Friendship grows like the flower that rests in our hand. But protracted delays or procrastination can lead to serious consequences that time and further endeavors cannot resolve. Pam's story illustrates this. Pam had many traumas of emotional abuse in her childhood and as a consequence became vulnerable to the negative influences of intimacy and attention. A friend connected Pam to her brother who had been serving time in prison. This introduction temporarily satisfied Pam's loneliness and yearning for attention and intimacy.

They communicated by mail and she became very loyal. Pam did not question the course of the relationship or its ultimate purpose until he asked her to marry him, approaching the time of his release from prison. She then became suspicious of his intention. She evaluated herself and recognized that she was overly loyal and patient to a man she really didn't know. Too much patience can delay our decision making and insight into an individual or situation. We lose track of time and become too loyal for the sake of it. Pam walked away from this relationship valuing her life in a much more meaningful way.

## Reflection:

Pam created an illusion with her patience. She was content for the sake of it and did not question her time spent until a rock fell on her head. It was his proposal for marriage. Pam had no interest. Too much patience enforces a fantasy land of peacefulness without a desire of confrontation. This can delay a wise decision because the mind and heart have not engaged with the exact expression of the moment.

Patience is an important act when it is in sync with the now. It reveals the radiance of the moment, the truth at its core. It also nurtures our wisdom to be with the I AM, the exact symbol and message. Patience unravels the truth.

The wisdom of patience believes that there is always a silver lining behind every cloud. This belief strengthens our faith with the unknown and infinite forces of nature.

Ralph Waldo Emerson …

Adapt the pace of nature: her secret is patience.

Patience nurtures us to embrace the now, the heartbeat of the moment. A rose will open and greet the blazing sun when the time is ripe and each rain drop will find its way to moisten the sacred land.

Mother Teresa once said…

Let nothing perturb you, nothing frighten you. All things pass. God does

not    change.    Patience    achieves
everything.

Patience trusts the moment rather than questions it. It is power in silence. A patient friend can sometimes learn more about us than we had ever discovered about ourselves. He or she is persistent and compelling with quiet gestures. A patient friend has an abundant heart, delves behind our mask, and unravels our character. He or she sees us as divine human beings and allows the steps of friendship to unravel on its own.

Lao Tzu once commented...

Nature does not hurry yet everything is accomplished.

## Joan's Story

This story illustrates why another client, Joan became impatient with the lack of upward mobility in her career. Many continuous disappointments had created a sluggish spirit and Joan lost her motivation until a kind friend listened attentively to her despair. This bonding experience calmed Joan's nerves and supplied spiritual nutrition to her soul. The more a good friend listens to our intimate story, the more we become able to see through the clouds and embrace the roots of our concern. Our whole being becomes lighter. We become more patient with ourselves and our spirit flows like the ripples of the water. We learn to patiently accept the divine timing of our life and realize that we cannot push Mother Nature.

## Reflection:

Joan learned the value of the higher order, the wisdom of the Creator. Her patient friend introduced her to the timing of life, Mother Nature. This is a deep lesson for all of us. We need never forget our partner, the Creator who has its own design for each of us. The more we acknowledge the Creator, the more we become patient because we know there is another force that is working with us.

There is nothing to rush except man-made time. The Creator has its own calendar.

A patient friend encourages us to follow our dream no matter how long it takes. He or she acknowledges the divine timing of the Creator more than the calendar that rests on the wall. He or she nurtures our spirit.

Each friendship produces a distinctive energy and pattern just as every artist creates a distinctive painting. The wisdom of patience discovers the I AM of a friend and respects each colorful story.

A Native American storyteller wisely commented...

Most of the time we are not patient enough to pay attention to the story.

Each friendship manifests a purpose in our lives and each friend lights our torch with each chapter in our journey. A patient friend believes that we are connected to the universal thread of humanity and that we all have an important story.

# THE SECOND AWAKENING

## THE PRESENCE OF LISTENING

*Big egos have little ears.*

— Robert Schuller

*A wise old owl sat on an oak tree*
*The more he saw the less he spoke*
*The less he spoke the more he heard*
*Why aren't we like that old wise bird?*

— Unknown

Listening creates a sincere and caring presence in friendship. Attention is given to our friend and these moments enhance a silent and profound bonding. Our friend feels comfortable to speak their truths without the fear of judgment and worry becomes lighter and more adaptable to healing the wounded soul. The presence of listening nurtures a warmth between two friends and the shadow of loneliness no longer punctures the wounded heart. A listening friend gives us their insight and compassion.

Mark Twain once wrote…

> If we were meant to talk more than listen we would have two mouths and one ear.

The presence of listening respects the spoken word as well as the moment of silence. It values dignity, patience, and the universal thread of humanity. Listening embraces the elements of life: the gentle rain drops that create serenity in our soul, rustling branches that sway to the dance of the wind, the birds that sing in the morning dew. Listening does not overlook the human elements nor the voice of nature. Patience is a virtue with the art of listening. The presence of listening enlightens us to our inner voice and the divine source.

Tagore once wrote…

Trees are earth's endless effort to speak
to the listening heaven.

A listening friend becomes our angel in disguise and
nurtures our soul as the rivers nurture the sacred land.
A listening friend strengthens our inner security. We
realize that we have a loyal and kind friend who
nurtures our heart like the opening petals of a
blossoming flower. He or she comforts us so that we
become more able to open up and more motivated to
address our past wounds, release them, and heal. The
support and attention that we receive from our friend
enables us to sing our own song and dance to the
rhythm of our spirit. He or she becomes our spiritual
healer who listens to our intimate stories and offers us
guidance along the many paths of our journey. We
develop more confidence pursuing our heart's desire
and fearlessly go forward with our calling. Our spirit
soars and the universe becomes an exciting adventure
filled with opportunities and colorful horizons.

This is a quotation from an unknown…

> The most basic and powerful way to
> connect to another person is to listen.
> Perhaps the most important thing to
> give to each other is our attention.

The Creator also listens to us and gives us synchronistic messages. The more we speak to the heavens with our prayers, the more we become aware of our spiritual partnership with the Creator.

Mother Teresa sheds this light...

> Before you speak it is necessary for you
> to listen, for God speaks in the silence
> of the heart.

## Cynthia's Story

Cynthia was challenged to learn about the presence of listening. She had been married for several years and had been in a roller coaster ride with her married boss, meeting him in his car during lunch hour. Her boss continuously told her that he had no intention of leaving his wife. She heard him but did not listen. It was easier for Cynthia to remain in an illusionary intimacy than to confront reality.

The biggest challenge for Cynthia was to confront herself, tackle her insecurities, and evaluate the relationship with the husband. She also had to delve into the reasons why she received more pleasurable enjoyment from her husband than her boss.

Later on, life gave her an opportunity. A door opened for her and it was up to her to walk through it. She did. A close friend, Allison, introduced her to horseback riding. This new outlet gave her much joy, clarity, and fulfillment. It allowed her heart to expand with dignity, self-respect, and self-empowerment. Her bonding with the horse manifested a powerful connection and allowed her to view her life in a larger perspective, like the infinite snowflakes that touch the moist ground. This passion created more meaning in her life and a new journey began. Her interaction with the horse enlightened her to value higher ideals and the horse became a good friend. She also began to listen to others enhancing spiritual and meaningful friendships.

Cynthia listened to her gut and realized that her marriage was also an illusion. She confronted her husband with courage in her heart and dissolved the relationship.

### Reflection:

Cynthia needed to engage with life on a larger scale and life gave her the opportunity. Passion speaks the truth in a very silent powerful way.

When we expand with our gifts, we expand with ourselves. We become more secure and comfortable with our inner being. We learn to love ourselves and are not fearful of confrontation. We become aware of our inner light and listen to our higher self. The presence of listening can do wonders for our soul.

It is a balancing act of the visible and the invisible, the duality of life. We become more balanced and connected to the spiritual law of nature, balance. We become one.

The more we connect to our passion, the more we will confidently go forward with the gifts given to us by the Creator. We will listen to the beat of our heart and this action develops into a healing process. The lack of listening to another human being or the lack of pursuing our innate abilities tends to confuse the expression of our spirit. We then become loyal to an unqualified situation or person. The presence of listening embraces the now.

This awakening engages with the heartbeat of our friend. Their story becomes our story and we realize that we all travel a universal path. They see through our shadow with acceptance and encouragement.

The following is a commentary from the book *Native American Wisdom*...

Traditionally, Indians did not carry out dialogues when discussing important matters. Rather, each person listened attentively until his or her turn to speak, and he or she rose and spoke without interruption about the heart of the matter under consideration. This tradition produced a measured eloquence of speech and thought that is almost unmatched for its clarity and simplicity.


## Jean's Story

Jean, a middle-aged woman, worked for a financial company, where her professional loyalty to her boss developed into a romantic friendship. During the course of time, her boss demonstrated intense outbursts of anger like bursts of fire. Jean maintained her loyalty despite his destructive behavior.

Sometimes anger is used as a defensive mechanism because the angry person does not want to listen to their inner thoughts and feelings. They also may not be comfortable or secure with themselves or their total essence, or they do not love themselves. Anger can be a "controlling" tool with no positive destination. It pops up and abruptly exits. The victim can become speechless and the body freezes.

The solar plexus or mid-section of the body is vulnerable and receives the flames of the dragon. The angry person does not allow the victim to speak and as a consequence the victim feels the lack of self-empowerment because of the shock of the experience. This can linger for several weeks if not released and healed. The presence of listening does not exist. Many intense emotions can distract the presence of listening. Listening is peaceful and connects to our higher self.

Her boss' angry demeanor deterred Jean from listening to herself until she received a revelation from her inner voice. Maybe this was an act of divine intervention, a message from the Higher Source who is watching over us. This wisdom motivated Jean to reflect on her life and take positive action, embracing her self-esteem and self-enlightenment. She became loyal to herself, listened to her heart, listened to her inner voice, and became a wiser human being.

## Reflection:

Sometimes loyalty distracts us from the act of listening. We wear sunglasses and do not allow the radiance of the sun to embrace us. We become loyal for the sake of loyalty and do not exactly know the reason. Too much loyalty limits our freedom and prevents us from making wise decisions.

All we need is a ray of sunshine to open our eyes to the truth. Then we begin to listen to ourselves and those around us. We listen from the depth of our heart and uncover all masks. We get to the depth of the soil and the depth of the heart.

We learn to appreciate silence, the silence of ourselves and the solitude of nature. The presence of listening respects all that is in front of one. It is a human element which connects us to life itself.

A listening friend can be as serene as a falling snowflake. Their presence of listening reflects admiration to us. They discover our inner self, which enhances a deeper dialogue in friendship and this creates more understanding and compassion.

This is a quotation by an unknown...

> A friend is someone who helps you when you are down, and if they can't they lie down beside you and listen.

Friendship will always have ups and downs, but its sincerity and strength will become apparent when two friends return to a mutual respect of listening, honoring each other despite a past windy storm. May we empathize with the joys and cries of our dear friend and listen to the depths of their hearts. This bonding creates a special trustworthy and intimate friendship. Our dear friend will open up to us like a blossoming flower that rests in our hand.

This is a quotation by another unknown...

> A friend listens to the song in my heart and sings it to me when my memory fails.

# THE THIRD AWAKENING

## COMPASSION

*Our task must be to free
ourselves by widening our
circle of compassion to
embrace all living
creatures and the whole of
nature and its beauty.*

— Albert Einstein

*Compassion brings us to a
stop, and for a moment
we rise above
ourselves.*

— Mason Cooley

Compassion is kind and empathetic to the struggles of mankind. The heart is full and willing to understand the commonality of all.

Seneca, a Roman philosopher, once reflected…

> Wherever there is a human being, there
> is an opportunity for kindness.

Compassion does not criticize another human being, because it believes that we are all connected to the Universal Breath of Life, the universal bloodstream of mankind. A compassionate friend nurtures us with their gentle warmth and delicate touch. He or she is genuine and humble enriching us with many fond and caring memories. Compassion engages spontaneously like a child that dances with no occasion.

Tagore, a poet, once commented…

> Every child comes with a message that
> God is not yet discouraged of man.

God has compassion for all and children remind us of the purity of love and their natural tendency for compassion. Children are the image of God. They intuitively know the act of giving in unpretentious ways and tend to be more other-oriented than self-indulgent. Children sincerely want to share and cooperate with their friends. This inspiration listens to the joys and cries of mankind. It is as deep as the majestic blue ocean and deeply embraces the heart of humanity.

An excerpt from Tamud…

> When a man has compassion for others,
> God has compassion for him.

A compassionate friend speaks straight from the heart and the intention is genuine. He or she is capable of peeling back all of our layers and soothes our soul with a bouquet of love. Compassion reaches out and honors the Oneness of mankind, the artist, the welder, the laborer, the teacher, the proprietor, and all souls created by the divine source. We are all One through the eyes of the Creator. We just have different resumes.

Mother Teresa once stated…

> Our sisters must walk the streets, take the street car as the people do, and enter the houses of the poor. We cannot enclose ourselves behind walls and wait for the poor to knock at our door.

A compassionate friend respects the differences of human beings. There is no loyalty to superiority because he or she affirms that we are all equally created by the Creator of Light. A compassionate friend offers guidance in our moment of grievance and confusion. The dialogue is gentle and does not infringe upon our freedom of decision-making. A compassionate friend does not judge our intimate story no matter how uncomfortable it is for us to express the difficult chapters of our lives. He or she understands that it is very easy to criticize a human being but it is very difficult to understand the plight of one's journey. No one can walk in our shoes or speak the beat of our heart. A compassionate friend becomes an angel in disguise and lifts our spirits to the heavens.

## The Servicemen's Story

This is another story about servicemen in combat and how their tender and poignant experiences strengthened their memories of friendship. These men bonded with each other in life-and-death events and never considered the belief of inequality toward their fellow man. They were all united with a common cause, defeating the enemy, taking risks, and deeply feeling for their fellowman with compassion. These powerful realizations also nurtured the blossoming of their humility.

They became the yin yang, the two spiritual poles of the spectrum, the female and male persona. Their emotions became very intense, like the depth of the powerful ocean. Their motivations and actions were warlike, like the warrior riding his horse seeking to conquer the land or anyone who interferes with his victory.

These servicemen sacrificed themselves for the survival of others without thinking of the consequences. The sacrifice for another human being is the depth of compassion. The heart unites with the heart of another.

Compassion nurtures a deeper insight, love, and wisdom with our family of friends. The servicemen learned this and much more.

### Reflection:

Compassion enhances human insight into our fellow man. It creates harmony and cooperation. It has the spiritual ability to bond to another human being because there is no evidence of separation or inequality.

Compassion is the voice of love to its highest degree. The act of compassion sacrifices without thinking twice. It is a spontaneous act that sings loud and strong.

Sometimes we need to be in a very intense experience to embrace compassion. The heart is challenged to deeply feel and the ego is dropped. We become one. Our heart becomes the heart of the other. This nurtures the awakening of humility. Compassion is the love of mankind.

The military men created meaningful friendships. They deeply felt the plight of their friend and this motivated them to automatically protect and defend their comrade. Their compassion was humanitarianism. They sacrificed their lives never doubting their action. Compassion is the human breath of life.

The Dali Lama once wrote...

> I truly believe that compassion provides
> the basis for human survival.

There is no role-playing with compassion. We connect to humanitarianism and recognize that we all breathe the same air and drink the same water. The eyes of the gardener are the eyes of the golfer, one spirit, one heart, and one blood stream. Compassion embraces all and is a positive force for humanity.

Leon Shenandoah from the Iroquois tribe once stated...

> I am working for the Creator. I refuse to
> take part in its destruction.

Compassion weaves all the threads of humanity. The more we believe that we are all One under the eyes of the Creator, the more we will intuitively extend our hearts to our neighbors, blood family, and our family of friends. The power of compassion constructs and does not seek to destroy. Compassion builds many human networks.

## Gabriel's Story

Gabriel had been abandoned at a young age by his alcoholic parents and as a repercussion was shuffled to many foster homes for battered children. These agonizing experiences influenced him to become streetwise and to adapt survival strategies like a hungry child who needs to figure out how to find food for his palate. Surprisingly, these dark experiences did not influence him to become a victim of anger and resentment towards his fellow man.

Gabriel became more compassionate with the struggles of mankind rather than internalizing personal negative feelings. He maintained his kindness and positive outlook towards life and was still convinced that there is a goodness in every human being. His ideals raised his perspective of humanity resonating to a higher spiritual level of consciousness. Gabriel chose to serve his fellowman and extend his heart in a qualified profession.

### Reflection:

Many of us have had to face very difficult and heart wrenching experiences. This can easily challenge our human qualities. Some of us become angry and resentful and question the why me complex. Others negate it and still maintain an inner peace.

Gabriel chose the latter. He was still convinced that there is still a goodness in every human being despite his extreme internal pain. He still felt for the other with an open heart.

The act of kindness is an art. It is gentle and intuitively does not infringe. It is peaceful and respects the heart of the other. One cannot have compassion without kindness.

Gabriel was open to life without discrimination. He did not allow the negative experience to stifle his spirit and used the experience to enhance his spiritual development.

Compassion breathes deeply, embraces all and loves with an open heart. It seeks to build human networks and is the image of humanitarianism.

Martin Luther King Jr…

> Life's most persistent and urgent question, "What are you doing for others?"

Sometimes our blood relatives substitute our need for building friendships and often supply us with false inner security. Our blood ties can limit our full expression to find our place and identity in the world. Friends can become more connected to our total presence because of the choices we make. This nurtures our heart which enables more vessels to open and we extend our compassion to our fellow man.

## Doctor O's Story

Doctor O diligently diagnosed the physical health worries of each patient as well as unraveling their lingering negative emotions. He believed that many physical illnesses are a result of emotional baggage that tends to get stuck in different areas of the body. He was not a mechanical doctor. He was a compassionate physician and throughout his practice learned that many patients needed the human touch as well as compassion to nurture the healing process.

He had the insight to see way beyond the physical illness and speak to the patient as a human being. They would feel better about themselves, acknowledging that they are indeed worthy to heal and that the disease was an opportunity to deeply learn more about themselves and those closest to them. Doctor O hugged his patients before and after the session, enhancing the human connection. The patient would leave the office feeling better about themselves, with hope and belief, as well as trusting that the doctor really cared for their welfare.

Many patients are vulnerable as soon as they walk into a doctor's office. They do not know what to expect and fear becomes a debilitating emotion. As a result, the patient becomes too frightened to ask meaningful health questions about their condition.

Doctor O encouraged his patients to ask questions so when they left the office, they were satisfied with their healthy dialogue. He did not need to advertise for patients. His compassion was his spiritual mouthpiece to increase his practice. Compassion nurtures the arteries of the soul.

## Reflection:

Compassion is a healing tool. It is a spiritual medicine and helps to heal those in distress. Dr. O displayed this with his patients. He believed that it is better for the patient to walk out of a doctor's office knowing that the doctor cares for the patient rather than the patient feeling a lack of care or comfort.

Patients are usually vulnerable as soon as they walk into an office. They expect a positive interaction and nothing can be as healing as a compassionate physician. This gives the patient hope and more of a willingness to live. A mechanical doctor does not tap into the heart of the patient and chooses to be aloof. But this can cripple the spirit of the patient. The patient needs to always feel as whole as possible and it is the responsibility of the physician to be as sensitive or compassionate to the patient. It is their duty to nurture the healing process with concern and wisdom. This can be a monumental task but it can be accomplished. This can become a healing process for the patient as well as the physician.

Compassion helps to soften unresolved negative feelings of a person because it accepts and encourages. This nurtures a healing process. Positive feedback is very important for the healing transformation. This can also manifest a deeper inner faith with the patient and this alone becomes a powerful healing agent. Any tool that enhances healing is a blessing to the health of the patient.

Dr. O believed in addressing the patient as a whole human being. Compassion was the healing tool for this insight.

A native Sioux once prayed…

> Great Spirit, help me never to judge another until I have walked in their moccasins.

Compassion increases our wisdom with life. We become more aware of the struggling stories of mankind and extend our hearts without seeking a reward.

The Dali Lama affirmed…

> If you want others to be happy, practice compassion. If you want to be happy, practice compassion.

The beauty of a compassionate friend is that another human being sees through the eyes of our soul with deep respect, insight, and the essence of love. The angels sing.

## THE FOURTH AWAKENING

## INNER SECURITY/INNER PEACE

*Work like you don't need money*
*live like you've never been hurt*
*sing as if no one can hear you*
*and dance like no one's watching.*

— Anonymous

*Everything has its wonders, even*
*darkness and silence, and I learn*
*whatever state I may be in, therein to be*
*content.*

— Helen Keller

Inner security creates an inner peace with ourselves and to those we cherish, our family of friends. A secure friend wants to share their experiences with us without fear or vulnerability.

A Native American once reflected…

Stand in the light when you speak out.

Inner security releases one's personal attachment to burdens or emotional diseases and trusts every step that the Creator provided, allowing each moment to develop to its total freedom. Inner security does not become troubled by a turbulent storm or treacherous waters. It embraces the now with a clear mind and resilient heart. Inner security is the embodiment of the I AM.

Mohandas Gandhi poignantly illustrated…

> Each time a man stands up for an
> ideal, or acts to improve… it is in itself
> part of the liberation and the foundation
> for inner security.

Inner security respects the natural timing of life and learns to adapt to its many twists without fear of the unknown. It walks the crooked path without the anxiety of a lurking shadow.

A secure-hearted friend listens to our concerns without projecting superiority or judgment. He or she walks besides us on each step of our path without motivation to manipulate our decision-making or demand an immediate response. There is no fear of confrontation. A secure friend recognizes that life will always give us different experiences to help us to grow wiser with each step along the way.

The following is a quotation by Seneca, a Roman philosopher...

> No tree becomes rooted and sturdy unless many a wind assails it. For by its very tossing it tightens its grip and plants its roots more securely. The fragile trees are those that have grown in a sunny valley.

## Brittany's Story

Brittany had been enamored with a spiritual leader for several years. He was in her eyes a perfect human being and could do no harm. Over the years, she became dependent on his counseling and repressed all avenues of attaining her own resolutions. Then a devastating event occurred in her journey and Brittany sought advice, comfort, and support from this spiritual leader.

She tried many times to reach him, but was only able to briefly speak to his assistant. This deliberate avoidance increased insecurities and anxieties because she had never been confident and comfortable with her own decision-making. However, this temporary negative experience provoked a positive twist, causing her to delve within the depth of her soul and transform into the sturdy oak tree. She connected to her inner strength, the nourishment of her spirit. Brittany realized that no one understands her life more than she does and began to cherish her freedom for decision-making. This self-awareness manifested a spiritual transformation in her life.

Dependency can sometimes cripple our inner security and weaken the ability to tackle the challenges of our lives. A dependent friend stifles our freedom with their consistent neediness to be with us and our spirit can easily become exhausted. The more Brittany confronted life's challenges, the more she became secure and peaceful with her decisions. She did not need someone else's approval and no longer placed anyone on a pedestal. Brittany became the empress.

## Reflection:

We can sometimes become over dependent on another soul in our lives which can lead to the loss of our independence, our freedom to think and feel with our truths. We disconnect from our inner security because we have chosen to depend on someone else. We forfeit our sense of peace because lack of one's security paves the way for anxiety and the fear of the unknown.

The fear of the unknown can create havoc to our soul. Our imagination can create stories that have nothing to do with the situation and this can become a whirlwind of confusion.

Security is believing in one's self, embracing our self-confidence and also acknowledging the higher power that has its own design. We can then become more assured with the unknown because we acknowledge the spiritual partnership that has its own way of speaking in a very silent way.

Brittany embraced her self-empowerment and her voice spoke the truth.

Willa Cather once reflected…

No one can build his security upon the nobleness of another person.

A secure friend enhances a healthy friendship and honors honesty, openness and cooperation. The more we confront a distressful experience, the more we will become aware of our courage and resonate with our inner security. Our eyes become wide open to exactly who we are in this present moment. We honor ourselves and take a bow.

Richard Evans once commented…

Don't let life discourage you. Everyone
who got where he is had to begin where
he was.

## Carole's Story

Carole struggled in her marriage for quite some time.
She had been extremely fearful of leaving her
husband even though he had offered to give her a
generous settlement. She heard but did not listen to
the truthfulness of his words.

Carole was insecure and uncomfortable with the
slightest notion of living with herself. Yet she was
already alone. Their communication had ceased.
Consistent socializing became her way of escaping the
reality of the marriage without any attempt of
confronting the problem. It was easier for Carole to
converse to others than to reflect on herself. She
needed an insightful and supportive friend who would
remove her rose-tinted glasses.

A friend appeared and did just that. He guided
Carole to take a leap forward, embrace her security,
and remove herself from the shallow marriage. She
did so, and became very content and peaceful living
alone. Her creativity blossomed, enhancing the artist
within. This creative and spiritual process enlightened
her to the depth of her self-identity, the I AM. This
client became secure in her full expression and
connected to the depth of her soul. She intuitively

followed the words of her gut, respecting her inner voice without hesitation. Intuition became powerful and meaningful, which also nurtured her sense of security.

**Reflection:**

Security rests with oneself and oneself alone. Sometimes we want to escape our lives without the interaction of it. We hear and do not listen. We do not want to go forward because we have created our own sense of an imaginary security, a comfort zone. The embrace of security can be very challenging to our total being. The more we feel our self-worth and our connection to the Source, the more we become secure with the choices in our lives. We confront ourselves and we confront life. We will never feel the sensation of loneliness. We have connected with our inner spirit and the inner voice of the Creator.

A secure friend will always want the best for us. He or she illuminates our soul with a thousand lit candles. A secure friend will nurture the growth and balance of friendship. Insecurity traps the spirit and tricks the soul. Our heart becomes paralyzed. Inner security embraces the now and the heart beats to its own drum. A secure friend freely speaks from the heart and nurtures the many passages for the awakening of friendship.

## THE FIFTH AWAKENING

## THE HONESTY OF COURAGE

*All our dreams can come true
if we have the courage
to pursue them.*

— Walt Disney

*I learned that courage was not
the absence of fears, but
the triumph over it.*

— Nelson Mandela

Courage is a light that glows in the darkness of every moment and fears are tossed into the wind. A courageous friend embraces the now and does not avoid speaking the truth in friendship. He or she speaks with an open heart and full spirit. The act of courage is filled with vitality, purpose, and fearlessness. It does not sabotage the steps leading to the intimacy of friendship. Courage nurtures sincerity without the fear of being vulnerable, intimidated, or rejected. A courageous friend gracefully unravels the silent burden of a friend and guides him or her to move forward with acceptance and self-worthiness. Courage is a spiritual warrior.

Tagore reflected…

> You can't cross the sea merely by standing and staring at the water.

Courage ignites any thoughts of resistance and is not fearful pursuing its goals. Courage has a vision and has dreams. It stirs all the molecules of our body. It is passionate with its action and goes forward with faith and hope.

Admiral Chester Nimitz once wisely asked…

> Grant me the courage not to give up even though I think it is hopeless.

Courage strives to attain its truth no matter what the obstacle. It does not refrain from the fear of the unknown and is loyal with its intention. Courage takes a risk without looking back and insecurity does not become a hindrance.

Mohandas Gandhi eloquently stated…

> There would be nothing to frighten you
> if you refuse to be afraid.

A brave friend forges ahead to reach the unthinkable and each new gallop reveals more strength that would never have been imagined. A brave friend is here for us through our difficulty and will not walk away. He or she will remain in the friendship and face our reality without illusion. Courage amplifies, magnifies and intensifies our reason of being.

Albert Einstein creatively suggested…

> Any intelligent fool can make things bigger and more complex. It takes a touch of genius and a lot of courage to move in the opposite direction.

Courage manifests transformation. It is the fuel that ignites the soul to overcome obstacles. A brave friend tells us the truth as well as applying truthfulness to themselves.

Christopher Reeve poignantly affirmed…

> I think the hero is an ordinary individual who finds the strength to persevere and endure in spite of overwhelming obstacles.

## The Freedom Riders' Story

Although they were not clients, they are so worthy to illustrate their monumental courage and love for humanity. These men and women sacrificed their lives, challenging segregation in interstate bus travel through civil disobedience. They embarked on a mission without the certainty that they would return home. Many had executed their wills because of the dreadful consequences that they would encounter. Their calling was to free blacks from injustice, and courage was their spiritual nutrition.

The Freedom Riders developed deeply fulfilling friendships during this human and political mission and fear did not block their goals. They courageously marched throughout many states voicing their convictions of freedom for all. They achieved many of their goals with courage as their spiritual ally.

Reflection:

Friendships develop naturally when men and women come together to achieve a higher purpose. It transforms into a cooperative calling and enhances a greater understanding and compassion with each other. Courage was the fuel for the Freedom Riders to go forward despite the horrific death threats along the way.

Courage mirrored the root of a sturdy tree that would not sway despite many an unknown storm. They were humble heroes.

Winston Churchill said…

Courage is the first of human qualities because it is the quality that guarantees all others.

Courage confronts life with all its ups and downs seeking a rainbow through the dark clouds. Courage is conviction.

Reinhold Niebuhr prayed…

God, grant me the serenity to accept the things I cannot change, the courage to change the things I can, and the wisdom to know the difference.

Sometimes illusion can distract us from the truth of friendship. An illusionary friend is not always sensitive to our distress because they are in their own bubble of being. He or she abandons the courage to speak out when there are intense differences and when feelings may become hurt. This lack of action enhances the insecurity of the friendship. A courageous friend deals with the situation and is not fearful of confrontation.

Joan of Arc proudly affirmed…

I am not afraid; I was born to do this.

## Jack's Story

Jack was a Cherokee who would walk barefoot during the time of the full moon and sketch a warrior prior to his hunting. He believed that the full moon manifested a lot of mystical energy like the blazing sun that magically warms our spirit. Jack believed that a ritual of acknowledging the power of the full moon with a combination of speaking to ancestors in the after-life would help him achieve his visions and dreams.

His persona transformed into the warrior while his spirit became as courageous as the lion in the vast woodlands. He spiritually connected to a tenacious image the warrior as well as recognizing the power of the other world.

Jack courageously combined the two spheres, the physical and the spiritual. He set his goals honoring the power of both worlds with no fear of the unknown. Courage was Jack's fuel for enlightenment.

## Reflection:

A courageous person acts with a strong belief system. They see beyond the now and seek to advance with their loyal dedication. Courage does not hold onto any fears in the past. Its spirit is strong and fearlessly moves forward on its path because of its strong commitment. It has a mission to succeed without giving power to any temporary obstacles.

Jack connected to his courage with his inner faith which gave more fuel to the fire. There were no conceived limitations in his world. A courageous person does not steer away from the attainment of its path. They believe and respect their mission.

The more courage we have, the more we are able to achieve. Fears may pop into our conscious mind or heart but they do not dwell. They do not take over our lives. They simply remind us that we are human and nothing is perfect. These dark invaders can also reinforce us to accelerate our courage nurturing a stronger belief system. Courage can be considered a framework for our self-growth. It is a powerful tool that enables us to open all doors.

Anais Nin once insightfully said…

Life shrinks or expands in proportion to
our courage.

**Peter's Story**

Peter drove cross country herding cattle for many
years. His beloved wife passed unexpectedly and
Peter was very much burdened with guilt because he
had concluded that he unwittingly chose his
profession over the care of his wife. This experience
affected him emotionally, creating more internal stress
with his profession. Later on Peter would feel the
presence of a spirit in his home and realized that this
spirit was his wife, and that her presence was there to
comfort him with the essence of love. The love of his
wife fostered an inner peace and he was able to
courageously release his past fears and guilt to the
wind.

Peter and other clients that received messages
from the other side revealed many fascinating stories.
Some would often smell perfume from their
deceased, listen to music that would start on its own,
see visions of loved ones at the base of their beds, or
watch objects moving without propulsion.
Peter became comfortable with messages from his
deceased wife. He became courageous with the
unknown and respected the two worlds.

**Reflection:**

It takes courage to recognize the unknown of the other side. Peter did just that and this awareness sparked him to abandon his present fears. His courage ignited him to rise above the occasion and embrace his inner faith. He did not attach any disbelief to the signs of the other side. He used them to his benefit recognizing that his loving wife was still with him in spirit.

Courage allows us to see beyond and to honor the unknown. It does not empower restrictions. It is a powerful force with no attachment to the past. Courage acts with freedom. It takes a courageous person to respect the symbols of the other side and feel comfortable with them. Courage recognizes and confronts the now. It does not hide behind closed doors. It wants to open them with a sensation of exhilaration.

The act of confrontation reveals the truth. It releases any questioning or wonderment. The courageous person delves into the depth of their heart and tosses away any fears into the wind. The gentle approach of confrontation is a gentle handshake and does not warrant any verbal fistfight. It seeks to unravel the truth no matter who the person is and is very comfortable with their action.

Courage is passionate. A courageous person could be a mountain climber, a sole proprietor, a person who moves cross country on their own, a sky diver, an artist who feels rejected with their work and still goes forward. Courage is independent of anyone or thing that interrupts the flow of ones person's belief system. It keeps on flowing and is confident with its rhythm. A courageous person does not allow fear to dominate their process.

A courageous friend will tell you exactly what is on their mind without the fear of confrontation. They are truthful with their words. There is no acting to please for the sake of it and will express their heart without anxiety or the fear of intimidation. The honesty of courage speaks its voice and is proud of it.

Courage initiates the way to a healthy transformation. It influences us to reach higher horizons without holding on to fears of the past. A courageous friend wants us to embrace our vitally and purpose. Courage awakens friendship to reach its highest means of expression. A courageous friend speaks from the heart without hesitation.

Lao Tzu reflected…

> Being deeply loved by someone gives you strength, while loving someone deeply gives you courage.

## THE SIXTH AWAKENING

## THE POWER OF FAITH

*Have faith in your dreams and some day
your rainbow will come smiling through.
No matter how your heart is grieving
If you keep on believing the dream
that you wish will come true.*

— Cinderella

*For all prayer is answered, don't tell God
how to answer it.*

— Anonymous

Faith honors the mysterious ways of the Creator and Its divine order. Faith does not question the mystical rhythm of the universe, the timing of the blazing Sun, or the cycles of the illusive Moon that touch the many heavens. It believes that a rose will always blossom in spite of a cloudy day.

The following is a Navajo song...

> Walk on a rainbow trail,
> Walk on a trail of song,
> and all about you will be beauty.
> There is a way out of every dark mist,
> over a rainbow trail.

The power of faith honors each divine moment without any recall. It listens to the messages of both the spirit world and the physical world because it believes that we are all connected by the Universal Spirit, the One.

Ralph Waldo Emerson observed...

> All I have seen teaches me to trust the
> Creator for all I have not seen.

Faith expands our beliefs, which are the nutrition for our inner security. It holds a belief in one's self as well as believing in the collective wisdom of our family of friends. We value our friends' decision-making and know that they are doing the best they are capable of at this time of their lives. Our blessings are with our friends through all their difficult times and their joyful moments. We recognize that life is a duality, a spiritual mixture of the shadow and the light.

A friend who has faith in us will want to guide us through our personal storm, believing that our perseverance will triumph and that we will embrace our inner light. They see beyond what we envision for ourselves because they have insight into us that we can never imagine. This awareness helps to develop our self-worth and self-belief. We become ready for the steps of inner transformation.

Sometimes we can easily become discouraged and lose the desire to go forward with our lives because of lingering unresolved scars that surface when we least expect it. Our vitality diminishes and our spirits become sluggish. Nevertheless, this meaningful occurrence can nurture reflection on our lives, leading to a deeper motivation for our calling. We fearlessly grab this experience with determination and belief that we can accomplish our heart's desire and have faith that our family of friends will also succeed with their vision.

Martin Luther King Jr...

> Faith is taking the first step even when
> you cannot see the whole staircase.

Sometimes our dear friend may not always be physically close to us. However, their spirit becomes intimate to our being, creating a powerful spiritual partnership. The spirit becomes magnified and bonding becomes real. We have faith with the powerful and intimate existence.

Friendships develop in a divine order that the Creator planned during the different stages of our lives. The manifestation of these friendships connects to our souls just as the universe manifests its miraculous plan with all the expressions of life. Each friend becomes a messenger that sparks the full extent of our soul's journey. Some friendships have many paths to travel, while some friendships may only have one lane. We nurture each friend to the best of our abilities, realizing that nothing lasts forever.

## Lisa's Story

Lisa had lived with an alcoholic husband for many years and became very depressed with the living situation. Nevertheless, she continued to believe she had a higher purpose in her journey and there was a light at the end of the dark tunnel. As time moved on, an inner light clicked within her conscious mind, enlightening her to the psychological, emotional, and spiritual damages within her marriage.

Sometimes in life we cannot always pinpoint or understand why a major shift occurs in the stages of our life. It can be divine intervention, an act from the Creator who forces us to leap forward even though we may never have thought of the idea. Lisa embraced the change, as she had always believed that the higher power was the conductor of the major shifts within her journey. This meaningful and unforeseen event increased her faith in the power of the unknown, the Force of light.

She left her marriage and reclaimed the beauty within her soul. Lisa pursued her ambition and decided to work as a counselor for women who lived in battered homes.

## Reflection:

Faith cannot be explained in words. It is a very powerful energy that silently guides us throughout our lives. It is our inner wisdom that can override all obstacles and can yet envision a rainbow through a turbulent storm.

Lisa always knew that she had a higher purpose in life. Sometimes we need to endure tough times to deeply delve and gain insight into the journey of our soul. These experiences can motivate us to become stronger and wiser with our mission in life.

Divine intervention is an act from the divine force. The Creator acknowledges what we are doing but nevertheless wants us to pursue another direction. It interrupts our flow either by creating an unexpected event or propelling us to think differently. This silent voice is our spiritual partner and ally that lurks behind closed doors. The Creator wants us to succeed with our calling and will do Its best to keep us on track. Divine intervention can give us many surprises. Our faith will embrace these spiritual jolts because we know it is for our highest good.

Faith is a silent word. Many of us have difficult obstacles to surmount. Faith becomes our survival tool for reaching a solution. Some of our friends have struggling experiences and the power of faith encouraged them to pursue their dreams and aspiration in spite of their haunting shadow.

## Dr. L's Story

Dr. L encouraged her patients to practice prayers and affirmations with their healing process. As a result, they recognized their self-healing and became their own best physician. Dr. L believed and witnessed the miracles of the human body affirming that the human spirit is the strongest energy force for healing. She had strong faith.

Her belief gave light to her patients, compassionately encouraging them to see within, to connect more to their heart, and to trust that every step has a higher purpose. They became elated with her wisdom and acknowledged the power of faith as one of the major tools for healing. Dr. L wanted her patients to believe that there is a strong hope for tomorrow and that they are quite capable to tackle the challenges that life gives them. The clouds will always come and go but the radiant sun will always shine.

Dr. L wanted her patients to believe in themselves no matter what their condition. Faith can change our perspective on life. It is a positive force that illuminates our body, mind, and spirit. Faith ignites us so that we believe in the power of ourselves and the spiritual partnership with the Creator.

## Reflection:

Prayers and affirmations can be wonder tools for healing. The patient acknowledges the importance of the higher power and speaks to it. There is no longer the unknown. It is known. There have been many studies on the power of prayers and all are good for the healing process. These tools contribute to the overall well-being of the patient, mind body and spirit. The heart becomes lighter and does not feel so burdened.

The more we use positive strong words, the more the heart becomes stronger. Our heart connects to the vibration and to the strength of the words. Our voice reflects the truth of our heart. A strong and pure voice speaks the truth. It is aligned with our body mind and spirit.

Dr. L strongly believed in the embrace of the known with the unknown, the duality of life, as well as its simplicity and complexity. She acknowledged the healing power of the physical world as well as of the spiritual world.

Helen Keller…

> No pessimist ever discovered the secret of the stars or sailed uncharted land or opened a new heaven for the human spirit.

The attainment of our gifts can become a reality with faith in our heart. We extend our expression for our own fulfillment as well as extending our blessings to our family of friends.

## Andrew's Story

Andrew had been a victim of a car accident and was brutally injured. He was pronounced physically dead upon his arrival to the hospital. During his transition to the other side, Andrew heard a god-like voice in the emergency room reminding him that his work was still not finished on the earth plane.

Life gives us many lessons for the attainment of our calling or mission. We are challenged to accept these lessons from the school of life. The more we follow and learn, the more we gracefully achieve the spiritual wisdom of life, faith.

If we do not learn from the lesson, life will give us the same lesson in another story, over and over again.

Andrew's spiritual adventure enlightens us to the presence of the Supreme Being, the producer and director of our journey. I believe that the major events of our lives will magically happen, and sometimes when least expected.

The less we attach ourselves to an uncomfortable experience the more we will connect to our faith. We will rise above the difficult situation, trusting its presence and increasing our faith with the Creator, our spiritual master.

Andrew recovered from his physical hardship and realized that he is never alone and that there is nothing to fear. He was blessed with the guiding light of faith and the essence of love.

## Reflection:

Sometimes we have to experience tragedy to connect to the voice of the higher power. Our faith becomes monumental for our survival tools. Andrew needed to experience a near-death experience to fully become aware of his need to fulfill his calling.

We are never alone. There have been so many stories of near-death experiences. It seems that we all have a mission and that we will not leave the physical world until our calling is complete. Many victims in a near-death experience have heard a voice which reinforces the need to go forward with their life in a more productive and thankful way.

Faith is magical. It is an awareness that life has its own order and rhythm. It has its own way which man cannot fully explain. The Creator is always with us. We just have to have the faith that it is the higher power that orchestrates our journey. We will then become free.

Faith is a meditative process that involves deep inner reflection. We need not think it. We believe and proceed. We have faith with the constant changes in our lives and accept the different tides that occur along the way. This enlightenment builds inner security, surrendering our ego and trusting the power of the unknown. We realize that there is a reason for every season and each friendship creates a powerful image in each stage of our lives.

Life is a continuous plan orchestrated by the Creator of Light. We do not always know the divine curriculum. Faith enables us to walk on many crooked roads. There are no dead ends. There are simply more opportunities.

We have faith that our friend will fearlessly open many new doors and encourage him or her to drink the glass of water even though it may not be filled to the top of the rim. We realize that there is no time table in the spiritual world and that our friend will learn life's lessons according to the divine schedule. We will continue to bless our friend believing that their life will unfold within the divine order. May we walk the many steps of friendship believing in its utmost power and possibility.

## THE SEVENTH AWAKENING

## THE GIFT OF GENEROSITY

*If we could have spared more,*
*we would have given more.*

— Canassatego Onondaga


*Give a bowl of rice to a man*
*and you will feed him for a day.*
*Teach him how to grow his own rice*
*and you will save his life.*

— Confucius

Generosity is a kind-hearted gesture that gives with sincere passion to help those in need. A generous friend gives for the sake of giving without looking back and seeks no reward. The heart is full like the Full Moon that radiates its glow to every spectrum of the universe.

Winston Churchill once observed…

> We make a living by what we get, we make a life by what we give.

A generous-hearted friend resonates with the gifts of humility, kindness, and compassion. The heart embraces the infinite expression of the Eternal Source, the endless moist land, the wide-open sky, and the impressive array of mountains. A generous kind-hearted friend will recognize the depths of our burden and will make no judgment or hasty resolution.

Henry David Thoreau reflected spiritually…

> The most I can do for my friend is simply to be his friend. I have no wealth to bestow on him. He knows that I am happy in loving him, he will want no other reward. Is not friendship divine?

A generous friend encourages us to constantly walk many pathways and connect to the image of our soul. He or she feeds our spirit with love. The gift of generosity has no other desire but to give.

Life challenges us with hardships and this can influence us to restrain from giving to those who are close to us, our family of friends. Our heart shuts down and this becomes a real challenge to maintain our generosity and comfort the tears of our friends with our support despite our own suffering. However, this adverse experience strengthens our character, increases our kindness with deep understanding and compassion.

Kahil Gibran once commented...

> You give but little when you give of your possessions. It is when you give of yourself that you truly give.

We were all created by the Eternal Source and this eternal light has no limitation. We can reflect on the infinite generosity of the Creator, the universal air that we breathe, the depth of the waters and the spacious heavens. We are all infinitely connected by a universal blood stream with infinite resources.

Martin Luther King Jr...

> Everybody can be great...because anybody can serve. You only need a heart full of grace, a soul generated by love.

Helping a friend nurtures their heart so that they no longer feel alienated or alone in the world. This gift nurtures our friend's inner security. A generous friend transcends the ego and gives spontaneously. They are unselfish with their time and give us the essence of love. The gift of generosity is kindness and compassion in action. It is patient and speaks to the heart of the matter.

Albert Schweitzer...

> Even if it is a little thing, do something for those in need of help, something for which you get no pay but the privilege of doing it.

Human stories educate and awaken us to the universal struggles of mankind, the universal tapestry of humanity. We learn from the simplicity and complexities of these stories and these stories stir our souls to acquire wisdom with the hardships of life.

Many of our friends have had painful experiences where they became too fearful and disconnected to heal themselves. A generous friend will give us quality time and patiently listen to our despair. They give us insightful feedback to our story and we become enlightened to ourselves.

## Lauren's Story

Lauren had been emotionally abused in her early childhood by her addicted parents. As a result of this trauma Lauren developed much more empathy towards the needs of children who lived in emotionally poverty-stricken homes.

Because of the impact of these intense heartfelt experiences, which pulsated deep in her soul, Lauren decided to gather investors to finance an arts center where children could express themselves without fear or insecurity.

During the process of any form of art, the artist connects to the depth of their soul and the spirit takes over. It becomes a therapeutic process, shedding healing light into every cell of the body. Art is beauty and mystical. The essence of nature is beauty and it has its own way of healing. Art therapy and drama were very helpful for Lauren in her earlier youth. She knew that she could express herself without the fear of vulnerability, and she felt safe in a loving space. Her expression became stronger like the brilliant rays of the yellow sun.

Many children burdened with hurtful events need to reciprocate to society with the gift of generosity. Their hearts are pure, vulnerable, and compassionate.

They feel from the heart, not think from the heart as many adults do. They are feelers and very intuitive. They are gifted little people.

Early childhood traumas can manifest in those with despair a new formula for looking at life, filled with streetwise wisdom. The child creatively looks outside the box because the interior needed new decoration. The child wants to feel a viable connection to a loving human being.

Friendships become more emotionally and spiritually intimate, enhancing more development for understanding and compassion. They give the gift of generosity without needing to take a bow.

## Reflection:

Early traumas in childhood can manifest both positive and negative experiences. The sensitivity of the child is raw and can easily ingest all of the toxic energies. This can then create a debilitation for the forward movement of one's life if the experience is not properly released and healed. It slowly grinds away at all of the cells, physically, emotionally, and spiritually.

Lauren did not embrace the above. She released the shadow and decided to devote herself to other victims in dire situations. Her heart expanded with loving thoughts rather than choosing to empower any darkness that would invade or stifle her total well-being.

Lauren empathized with others in hardships and this self-awareness paved the path for the enhancement of kindness and generosity. She knew that she needed to serve mankind. Her blood relatives did not serve her needs and this recognition increased the desire for meaningful human relationships or friendships.

Many leaders in all fields of life have had tragedies in their earlier years. It was almost as if it was meant to be, an event to produce tools for survival and leadership. This hardship motivated them to lead and nurture mankind. They had more of a desire to connect to humanity, a compensation for their earlier years. They became generous with their time and the expression of their hearts was truthful. These men and women did not need to "control" or manipulate another human being. They gave generously. This was their gift to mankind, the gift of generosity.

Children can teach us many lessons about the gift of generosity. Children have not yet learned role-playing and reach out to their friend with trust, little discrimination, and a pure heart. Their arms are wide open. Children tend to bond easier than adults. They nurture friendship on a very deep human level. Children do not hold onto grudges as in the adult world, they bounce back quicker, and they give more freely. They tend to be more intuitive than adults and sense the goodness of another human being and give straight from the heart. Children are wise little people.

**Eve's Story**

Eve became very reflective about the disbursement of her financial estate and she discussed this important contemplation with many of her friends. She learned that they had already planned to allocate their assets to their blood relatives, even though these blood ties were all financially stable.

It seemed to Eve that her friends were looking inside the box, re-establishing the security of their blood ties, as opposed to looking at friends or others in hardship situations.

With much deliberation and soul-searching, Eve decided to donate all of her assets to a children's charity dedicated to the research and cure of life-threatening diseases. Writing a check still did not satisfy her generous heart. She needed to feel the human, spiritual connection and later volunteered her services, the gift of generosity.

### Reflection:

It is very easy to write a check to a cause. But when we volunteer our services and invest our time with a charity, we become truly involved with its mission. We identity with it and learn about its many generous ways that it serves mankind. We become more compassionate.

We open our hearts and give like the river that continuously flows despite any protruding rocks along the way. A generous friend gives like the ripples of the water that infinitely flows.

A generous-hearted friend elevates our spirit. The friendship becomes humble, human, and truthful. The heart of friendship is pure and gives for no other reason than for the desire of giving. Our dear friend becomes memorable to us with their spontaneity and sincerity. We bless them and our heart rejoices.

## THE EIGHTH AWAKENING

## GRATITUDE

*Count your blessings instead of your crosses;*
*Count your gains instead of your losses.*
*Count your joys instead of your woes;*
*Count your friends instead of your foes.*
*Count your health instead of your wealth;*
*Love your friend as much as yourself.*

— old proverb

*A single grateful thought*
*raised toward Heaven*
*is the most perfect*
*prayer.*

— Gotthold Ephraim Lessing

Gratitude resonates with the flavor of humility, gentleness and kindness. A grateful friend does not assume or take anyone or anything for granted. He or she appreciates how precious life is and how each moment is worth much more than we can ever envision.

Ken Keyes Jr. once wrote...

> To be upset over what you don't have is
> to waste what you do have.

Our eyes become wide open when a friend listens to us through our difficult times and we appreciate them for their time and patience. We bless their presence. Gratitude is in the now without the attachment of the past memory. It opens many portals of self-discovery. Gratitude loves all the elements of life.

Robert C. Savage alludes...

> The richest person is the one who is
> contented with what he has.

Life will always challenge us with many distressful lessons that we can never fully anticipate in our worldly agenda. However, temporary obstacles can activate our perseverance, which can then develop our innate character, wisdom, and zest for living. A good friend is with us through these internal battles and supports us with compassion and conviction. We will remember their loyalty, respect, and empathy during the perils of our lives and we become more grateful with sincerity. These supportive experiences manifest powerful memories in our heart. We resonate to them as our family of friends.

## Doug's Story

Doug had been diagnosed with a life-threatening disease. Nevertheless to say, Doug had never expected such a physical or emotional suffering. His lifestyle came to a halt. Doug was challenged to deeply delve into his spiritual tool kit for his survival. His faith became the fuel for his spirit to confront life for all rainy days. It was his inner medication.

He became enlightened and grateful to his family of friends, who had extended their support and comfort during these moments of peril, enriching fond and satisfying memories.

The perspective of his life changed. As a consequence of this awakening, small stuff no longer rented any space in his brain. His calling became activated like the dormant clouds that break into a heavy downfall. His spirit became more vital, confronting all roads of life without hesitation.

Doug became very grateful for the friendships that did not waiver in their integrity and relentless love. Those friends contributed to his healing, feeding him spiritual nourishment and nurturing him to confidently open doors in his life. Gratitude is an award in silence.

## Reflection:

Life-threatening experiences such as health or war-survival tactics force us to dig into our core, our soul, our spirit, and our character or inner essence. These jolting experiences manifest a powerful spiritual transformation. They challenge us to engage with a life decision, to embrace life with a higher conviction or walk away with no attached responsibility.

Usually, we want to go forward because we have become more aware of exactly who we are. The I AM and this pride reaffirms in us a deeper desire to live and never take life for granted. We become more grateful for our existence and for those that became our angels or our family of friends. We bless them and we are grateful.

Robert Kennedy observed…

> We must find time to stop and thank
> the people who make a difference.

We are all children of the Creator and this awakening opens many doors for our spiritual growth. This enlightenment ignites the beauty of humility. Humility gives us the insight to see beyond the physical realm of a friend. We embrace their concern with no sense of superiority. Each friend who walks in our path can be a messenger for the Creator, directing us to our self-discovery through every dimension of our journey. A good friend encourages our special gifts to blossom because he or she truly believes in us. Our dear friend can become our spiritual coach or mentor who sheds light on the many paths of our way.

Albert Schweitzer...

> Sometimes our light goes out but is blown into flames by another human being. Each of us owes our deepest thanks to those who have rekindled the light.

Our family of friends becomes the gatekeepers to our heart. They nourish our soul with kindness. On the other hand, emotional burdens can limit a friend's expression of gratitude to another because of the scars that contaminated their heart and stifled the vitality of their spirit. They become unable to recognize the goodness of a friend and intimacy becomes skewed.

**Maria's Story**

Maria had never been satisfied with the passages of her life. She wanted each step of her life to be orchestrated the exact way that she had wanted it.

There was no opening for flexibility. Maria ran a tight ship. She became angry with life and could never understand why everything that she had wanted took so long to accomplish. Many times she would become frustrated and released her anger towards her family of friends without any logical reason.

Maria never wanted to smell the roses along her road trip of life. It took too much time. She needed to appreciate the essence of the now, the texture of the petal, the softness of its touch, its beauty and enchantment.

The more we want things our way now, the less we see, feel, and listen, and the more we are eager to criticize our fellow man, our friends. We never learn to appreciate our friendships because our ego is too involved with our own needs.

Life gave Maria a lesson on gratitude. A close friend suddenly passed and this sadness deeply pierced her heart. She became ill with despair. This alarming experience jolted her psyche to reflect, to meditate on her life in a very different way. She realized that all events do not need to occur so quickly and that life has its own way of nurturing the moment. Maria had thought that she was always in "control" of life until a dear friend enlightened her to one of the many lessons of life: You cannot push

Mother Nature but must respect its natural timing. A plant will always grow on its own accord. She became freer with this wise lesson, less hostile, and much more peaceful. Maria enriched her life with gratitude.

## Reflection:

Anger can be spiritually damaging to our body mind and spirit. It is an outburst without a higher spiritual purpose and verbally attacks with the sense of righteousness. Anger can easily debilitate the spirit, which in turn creates toxins in one's heart. An angry person displays outbursts and usually walks away without facing any responsibility for their actions. Nor do they acknowledge that they may have deeply hurt a person. Anger is an emotional hurricane.

The more one becomes aware and sensitive toward other people, the more one will hold off anger. The person will think twice before hurting someone or igniting a stressful situation. It is very difficult to embrace gratitude with the emotional knots of anger. The heart has to go through spiritual cleansing and release its resentments and frustrations, whether it be in the conscious or unconscious mind. We then become healed through this transformation and a new freedom exists within our total being.

The more we become free and embrace our inner peace, the more we become clearer with our lives and those close to us. We learn to be grateful for the steps of life that the Creator has given to us. We do not need to steer or "control" each step along the way. We accept the silent voice of the Creator and realize that life is a balancing act. We are grateful for the known in our experiences and have faith in the unknown. We do not become angry when we do not achieve something and do not display anger to a dear friend without any rhyme or reason.

We embrace our present friends and look forward to the unknown of others who will appear along our way. We are grateful for our family of friends. We bless them.

Children can teach us lessons about this dilemma because their hearts are relatively pure. Friendships are very important to them, especially to children of all types of struggling backgrounds where there is a lack of emotional encouragement and stability. These children embrace the awakening of friendship with a deep gratitude because they need to feel connected and accepted by another human being. Their friends fill a supportive and spiritual gap that had been vacant in their home and as a consequence they become very appreciative of friendship without discrimination.

Life is a school to learn our spiritual homework and we become more evolved when we learn the difficult lessons. We do our homework, cross the finish line, and attain wisdom. We connect to our self-love and express our colorful spirit in a way that an artist paints their fullest expression on canvas.

Nothing is more meaningful than the awareness and excitement of our inner being.

We learn to enjoy the simplicities of life and extend our heart to our supportive network, our family of friends. They fill our hearts with happiness. Gratitude teaches us to appreciate our friends in a very real and insightful way.

Let us envision friends holding hands as brothers and sisters with the self-awareness that we are universally connected in the eyes of the Creator. Gratitude accepts the present moment without question. Gratitude embraces the moment which is connected to the Divine Source.

Marcel Proust once observed...

> Let us be grateful to the people who make us happy; they are the charming gardeners who make our souls blossom.

## THE NINTH AWAKENING

## ESSENCE OF LOVE

*This is my beloved and this is my friend.*

— Song of Solomon

*Open your hearts to the love God instills.*
*God loves you tenderly. What he gives you*
*is not to be kept under lock and key, but*
*to be shared.*

— Mother Teresa

Love is the most delicate of our emotions. It is a continuing running brook that nourishes the very depth of our soul. The essence of love is beyond words. Its greatest and most touching means of expression is for the love of mankind with compassion as its fuel.

A loving friend nurtures our heart in a very magical way. He or she embraces us with their kindness, acceptance, and deep understanding. A loving friend sacrifices time for us. They encourage us and we attain more confidence in fulfilling our calling no matter how many temporary obstacles greet us along our way. This act of empathy creates within us a spiritual transformation which taps into our inner light.

Victor E. Frankl once wrote…

> Love is the only way to grasp another human being in the innermost of his personality.

Love is not demanding and does not seek to change one's personality. It is a beam of light that shines throughout our entire spirit. Love is a natural and powerful energy much more than words can ever describe. A loving friend nurtures us in a way that helps us to unfold and expand with the many layers of friendship. The spirit of love is young and has no limitations, like a child who sings and dances with no occasion.

Love resonates with its different faces, from a child's innate ability to love to the tapestry of humanitarianism. The more the heart expands, the more it will touch other people with compassion, which can be seen as the highest expression of love.

A Greek proverb…

A heart that loves is always young.

A loving friend helps heal our past toxins and opens the vessels of our heart. They have the capacity to cleanse our past traumas with their grace of forgiveness and acceptance. The love of a friend is the spirit of the Creator. Love does not control another human being because the more one controls the less one loves. The essence of love is not self-oriented. It is other-oriented and keeps on reaching out to the hearts of many.

It does not manipulate to serve its own purpose. Love merges with another human being and does not forfeit insight with its own self-identity. On the other hand, humanitarian love merges with the collective spirit of mankind to express universal ideals that serves the higher spiritual purpose of humanity.

Friendship bears no role playing. It is honest and genuinely loving. A loving friend medicates our soul with the spiritual tools of patience and the willingness to understand just who we are without bias. They want the best for us without the drive of competition. Their love embraces us and captures ones heart with a sense of inner security and peacefulness.

Kahlil Gibran once commented…

Love has no other desire but to fulfill itself.

**Valerie's Story**

Valerie had contemplated suicide many times because of the overwhelming events that had overburdened her life. She became lifeless and had no desire to interact with other people. Valerie's persona transformed into a crab developing a very hard protective shell. She had lost her fighting spirit.

Friendships became her saving grace during her intense depression. These loving friends were there for her without the acknowledgement of a time table.

They graciously sacrificed themselves all for the healing of Valerie and shed bright light with the rays of love, hope, and compassion.

These dear friends had the insight that everyone in life has a history to bear and that understanding ones background enhances the capability to nurture, respect, and heal a friend in the present.

Her friends became her angels or spiritual counselors better than any prescription a doctor could possibly prescribe.

These loving friendships manifested a healing therapy for Valerie. The events in her life, small or large, did not become as monumental and Valerie was even able to express humor. Loving friends became healers to every cell of Valerie's total being. Her emotional injuries became lighter, opening the door for self-love. The essence of love is as powerful as the majestic mountains, strong as a tidal wave, and as gentle as the blue eyes of an infant resting in ones arms.

## Reflection:

Compassion, the greatest human experience for love, is honest, empathetic, and truly loving. It does not waiver. It is there. A compassionate friend fills us with their heart and even more. Compassion is as deep as the ocean and fills the many horizons of the turquoise sky. It speaks from the heart with the golden words of truth.

Love is a healing nutrient. When we are with true love, we are with the truth of life. It is the essence of every living force created by the divine force of life.

A loving friend is with us in spirit. We can feel their presence even if they are not physically with us. Their love is connected to us by a silver chord or the echoes of life. A loving friend creates more healing to our total being than a thousand pills. They connect to our heart and the heart is where our emotions are stored. It is the most sensitive organ. A loving friend helps to heal our heart because love allows us to be exactly who we are without judgment or criticism. It does not seek to manipulate. It seeks to understand.

Valerie was very vulnerable because of her desire to commit suicide. Her willingness to live was very limited, nor did she value or appreciate her life. She needed to feel that life was worthwhile.

Friendships helped the healing process. She felt the love and this nutrient gave her food for life. She did not feel as overburdened and as a result of this awakening, she became much lighter with her thoughts. Her life did not seem as severe. Love eased it. Her loving friends gave her a sense of hope, inner faith and self-love.

A loving friend can help heal many wounds. It does not puncture the scar. It helps to heal and allows time to take its course. A loving friend taps into our heart, nurtures our spirit, and allows us to sing and dance to the voice of our soul.

We learn from our past friendships and these memories help us create our love formula for future friendships. Each friend that enters into our journey enlightens us. They become our spiritual messengers with each path that we were led to travel. We learn to delve into ourselves and become aware of how we truly prefer to be loved and we integrate this love formula with each new friendship. Our loving friend becomes our angel and we feel blessed.

Martin Luther King Jr…

> If you are seeking the highest good, I
> think you find it through love.

Love is an everlasting light that nurtures the unceasing existence of all things in the world. The expression of nature blossoms with its own timing like the blossoming steps of friendship.

Native Chief Dan George…

> For man must love all creation or he will
> love none of it.

Many times in our lives a difficult situation hinders our engagement with love. These experiences challenge our love formula that has not yet been developed, respected, nor valued. Some of us became emotionally attached to a hardship while others rise above it with faith and self-love. We continue to extend our love in friendship because throughout our struggles we developed more humility, compassion, and grace. Intense difficulties create opportunities for wisdom and awaken us to the universal thread of humanity.

Each friendship beholds its own rhythm like all the breathing elements of nature. The heart has its own timing and rhythm when it expands with love. Some friendships develop slowly over time. Other friendships blossom instantaneously and other friendships are deeply connected because of the many past lives and karma that need to play themselves out.

The more we evolve with our love formula the more our friendships will mirror exactly the love that is needed for our lives. We become the White Light that shines its love to our friend and we also extend our compassion to the many hardships of mankind.

An Apache quotation…

It makes no difference as to the name of the God, since love is the real God of the world.

**Rose's Story**

Rose's friend Karen was always very pleasant to her, especially when her husband was nearby. She had served Rose a lot during Rose's severe illness. I believe serving is a cerebral form of attentiveness and could even include loyalty, while giving resonates from the heart without any thought process. The person gives because the heart feels and sympathizes with the other.

The "friendship" seemed to be peaceful, without signs of provocations. Rose needed to be stress-free and to peacefully heal.

Then an irate incident occurred and Rose was taken ajar. Karen impulsively exploded like the roar of buffaloes, screeching not screaming, pointing a finger at Rose, criticizing her, and even alluding that she had not been to the home for several years and now she decides to stay even though it was for recovery. This devastating event continued for approximately 15 minutes, Karen's body quivering while screeching directly into Rose's face.

It became apparent that Karen had repressed her innermost emotions toward Rose and the truth came out while the husband was not around. This verbal attack devastated Rose, her body froze and her voice became speechless. After the forge of criticisms, Karen returned to her room without an apology and continued her "normal" routine. She never acknowledged her display of disrespect or the pain she inflicted.

This emotional rape debilitated Rose for several weeks because her body was so raw from the physical treatments. Her emotions needed to be healed and loving friends walked her through the process of healing with compassion. Rose needed to release the damaging toxins and continue her healing process.

Rose had approached Karen the next day addressing her angry behavior and Karen's response was that Rose was also screeching. She also tried to defend herself by claiming that this type of incident only occurred once. This was one time too many for Rose, who needed to be healed.

At that moment the friendship ended for Rose. There was no trust, respect, or the awakening of the essence of love a magical force emanating from the Creator. The essence of love is pure, compassionate, truthful, and glows from the heart. It does not hold onto other stuff that complicates the essence of giving. It does not twist words or manipulate all for the sake of attaining power and control.

Love flows with the tides, gives for the sake of giving and genuinely appreciates a friend with love in one's heart. It can move mountains and open many hearts. It is a white light, pure and healing.

## Reflection:

To serve one is very different than to love one. Both are to be respected and both suggest a higher purpose. But it becomes an irresponsible endeavor when the person gives and is not truthful with themselves. They extend themselves with the action of serving the other and at the same time repress their negative feelings towards the other. They become mechanical beings rather than expressing the voice of their heart.

Karen's repressed feelings exploded with frustration, insecurity, and anger. Her heart did not consider the feelings of Rosie. It never entered her mind that she could have deeply hurt Rosie especially in the healing time of her life and walked away without an apology.

Karen also never addressed her screeching issues. We do not spiritually grow when we do not have the courage to look at ourselves. It takes fortitude to acknowledge that we need to refine our character in order to spiritually and emotionally grow. We then become the plant that will blossom despite a windy storm.

The essence of love gives freely from the heart. It has no agenda because it is a natural act like the ripples of the water that continually flows. It is not ego based. It is other-based and is willing to sacrifice when need be. It is real, truthful and honest. The essence of a loving act stems deeply from the heart. It is compassionate that seeks to understand the other without criticisms. It gives for the desire of giving.

My take on forgiveness:

We have all heard the word and I have reflected on its meaning on many an occasion.

I do not always believe that we have to automatically forgive the person once they have deeply hurt us. I do not think forgiveness should be an automatic gesture. It should be a word for reflection and understanding. Automatic forgiveness can also enable the person to exercise the same action even more so if that person has not yet evolved.

I prefer the word "understand." Maybe we need to gain insight into their action and learn wisdom from it. To understand the action sparks more wisdom to our soul.

Karen had deep anger issues and was not able to confront her truest feelings. She took it out on an innocent vulnerable victim. Perhaps there were competition issues that she had never confronted. The derogatory words was her method of "controlling" or manipulating the space on her premises. I do not think that forgiveness is applicable with this situation because she still thinks that her action was "right". We hope she will evolve.

The Loving Creator is always giving us lessons and we need to embrace them and ride with the tide. There was a very big lesson for Karen which was to recognize her toxic behavior that she inflicted on Rosie as well as coming to terms with herself. This reflective journey will enhance self-growth and spiritual transformation which will allow the essence of love to embrace every cell of her body.

The Creator is always in our hearts and the spirit of love speaks loud and strong. Love is as peaceful as the blades of grass that sway to the music of the gentle breeze. It releases all shame and guilt, accepts one's weaknesses and fears. The more we release our lingering fears, the more we become whole and our heart travels to many lands. Love regenerates itself moment to moment from a higher source which is the force and nutrition in each cell and every DNA of our body. The spirit of love is the voice of the Creator and the Creator is rooted in each and every one of us.

May each friendship blossom like the rose that rests in our hand.

-----Carol Olivia Adams

## WISDOM OF PATIENCE

I know that the Creator is present
The Creator is patient with me
I respect the wisdom of patience
I allow the timing of life to be
I follow the steps that the Creator
Has given to me

Patience
Realizes that life has a master agenda
I AM patient
With the timing of my life
I love life

Patience evolves
Patience transforms
Patience allows the truth
To be seen
To be heard
To be free
Patience teaches me
The truth of my life

## PRESENCE OF LISTENING

I see the light in a friend
I listen to the voice of their spirit
I embrace my friend through the silence of listening
I embrace my friend with love
I love my friend

I AM with the silence of the Creator
The Creator gives me inner peace
I AM with my true self
I listen to my inner voice
I love myself

I listen to my friend
Because I care
My friend listens to me
We listen to each other
We speak in harmony
We listen from the depth of our hearts

## COMPASSION

Angels listen to our voice
Angels vibrate to our soul
Angels sing the song of compassion
The song of compassion is love
May mankind elevate their heart and join
The song of compassion

I honor the universal thread of mankind
My heart echoes the spirit of compassion
I am one with mankind

Compassion connects to the universal thread of
humanity
Compassion touches the depth of the soul
And deeply seeks to understand the other
Without judgment
With only love

## INNER SECURITY/INNER PEACE

The Creator loves me
I AM secure
I embrace myself
Security rests within me

I walk with the presence of the Creator
I listen to the presence of the Creator
I feel the presence of the Creator
The Creator is my partner
I AM with my inner peace

Security
Gives me
Total freedom
To be who I AM
Rich in spirit
To walk freely
To speak without hesitation
I AM secure with myself
I cherish my inner peace

## HONESTY OF COURAGE

Courage is the drum beat in my heart
Courage is my spiritual fuel
Courage travels many adventurous roads
Courage seeks to succeed
With a strong conviction

I have the courage to take risks
I will try my best
To try my best
Is success
I have courage

Courage believes in a dream
Courage does not give up with the attainment of a
dream
Courage speaks wisely
And acts justly

## POWER OF FAITH

Speak to me Creator
I will listen to thee
I will listen to the signs that you
Graciously send to me
Speak to me Creator
I will listen to thee
I will follow your way
I know that your heart is with me

I have faith with the timing of the Creator
I move forward with faith in my heart
I have faith that the Creator will reveal to me
The messages of each step of my life
I know that all is orchestrated with the divine rhythm
I have faith with my life
I have faith with the Creator

I have faith that I will attain my highest purpose
I realize that life will give me many challenges
I honor the lessons to be learned
I have faith that I will achieve my divine calling

## GIFT OF GENEROSITY

The Creator is abundantly generous
And is the source of life
Without boundaries
I respect our spiritual partnership
I will generously give to mankind
I will be generous with my friend

Let us hold hands with love in our hearts
Let us voice our compassion to humanity
Let us honor the universal thread of mankind
Let our generosity be our guiding light

Bless the gift of humanity
Knowing that helping others is an act of love
An act of kindness
An act of grace
An act of generosity
Bless the act of giving
To our dear friend

## GRATITUDE

I AM grateful for my gifts
I will share my gifts to humanity
And
To my family of friends

I embrace the wisdom of the Divine Source
I realize that a detour can create a
Deeper understanding for my journey
I walk each new path with gratitude in my heart
I am grateful for my life
And will do my best with each new direction that the
Creator has given to me

I am grateful for the given paths of my life
I am grateful for the family of friends that have
Joined me along the way

## ESSENCE OF LOVE

The Creator is the nurturer of my soul
The Creator nurtures the essence of a rose
The Creator feeds the root of a tree
The Creator is the rhythm of life
The heart of the Creator is love

Love is gentle
Love comforts the soul
Love is abundant
Love heals
Love is the essence of the Creator
Love encompasses all

I love
I AM one with the Source
I AM love

# Carol Olivia Adams

Carol Olivia Adams — inspirational writer, professional intuitive counselor, lively guest on cable TV, and former host of the inspirational radio show Intuitive Carol and Healers — gives us insight into spiritual and humanistic principles in *The Awakening of Friendship*.

As radio host, she revealed the wisdom of each practitioner to provide listeners with guidance on how to elevate their consciousness, magnify their spirit, liberate themselves, and attain their calling.

Carol Olivia has learned throughout her many intuitive sessions with clients the spiritual value of her patient ear, kindness, and sincerity, blending with each session her wisdom of spirituality, her background in psychology, and plain common sense.

Many universal principles of humanity became apparent in her healing profession and these principles inspired Carol Olivia to delve and recognize the human connection of friendship with greater understanding and deep appreciation.

This self-realization became the catalyst for *The Awakening of Friendship*, the acknowledgement of the human and spiritual connection of friendship enhancing the golden thread of dignity, respect, and compassion. Some of these awakenings, which she had become aware of during healing sessions with clients, are courage (the ability to fearlessly speak the truth in friendship), presence of listening (honoring the spoken word of a friend), compassion, and the wisdom of patience (allowing the developmental steps in friendship to unfold like the petals of a blossoming flower).

Carol Olivia Adams has been seen on cable television and other radio programs and will continue media interviews, public speaking, and lecturing. She can be contacted at carololivia7@gmail.com. Her website is www.theawakeningoffriendship.com.

Made in the USA
Middletown, DE
13 November 2015